D0053978

Mary's Lavish Gift

The Practice of Anointing with Oil

Wm I. "Bill" Edmunds

Mary's Lavish Gift
The Practice of Anointing with Oil

Every Good Gift
P.O. Box 130240
Houston, TX 77219
www.everygoodgift.com

ISBN 978-0-9785677-0-5

Printed in Korea

Preface

"We are excited and blessed that you have an interest in Anointing Oil. As Owners and Directors of 'Oil of Gladness' we are passionate about the use of Anointing Oil as a symbolic aid for prayer and ministry."

Oil of Gladness was founded in 1990 with a mission to serve the local Christian bookstore by providing high quality oils and allied products. We now sell to about 10 nations including the U.K., Holland, & Canada. We are also serving our military through the chaplaincy of the various branches.

It is our prayer that this book will both instruct and inspire you as you continue to serve our wonderful Lord Jesus and minister in His Name.

He Reigns!

Michelle & Marlin Zwicky

Acknowledgments

Our heartfelt thanks go to the team of people who each have made a contribution to enable this book to be in your hand right now.

W. I (Bill) Edmunds the author, whose thorough research, life experience and well chosen words form the backbone of this book.

Dotty Collins our long-time friend and awesome woman of God for her skilful scrutiny of words, grammar and punctuation.

Pastor C. Neil Sayers our Editor, friend and author of the devotionals of Family Fullness Ministries for 'bringing it all together'.

Zack Zwicky our son, for his graphic arts talent and heart to be a part of God's work.

Our customers – both retail and wholesale for their faithful business support and commitment to God.

Finally to you the reader: we prayed for you long before you read these pages. Our hope is that the Lord would use this book both to inspire and instruct you. We are honored you have this little book in your hand.

Anointing Oil - a brief history

In ancient times, olive oil mixed with fragrant herbs and spices was commonly used, not unlike the perfumes, ointments and creams of today, as a means of refreshing or invigorating the skin *(Ruth 3:3; 2 Sam. 14:2; Ps. 104:15, etc.)*. This custom is continued among Arabs and Palestinians to this day.

Making anointing oils and perfumes available to arriving guests was an expected act of hospitality. Unpaved roads, little more than rock strewn paths, exposed travelers to harsh conditions and much dust and grime. The crude sandals of the day offered little protection to travelers' feet. Custom required that every host receiving visitors must provide a basin of scented water for washing. Wealthier homes had servants assigned to wash the feet of those who entered – a task relegated to the lowest in rank of the household. In addition to washing the feet of each guest, the servant would also anoint their heads with sweet smelling oils or perfumes. This was the scene played out in the home of a Pharisee who took objection when a woman of the street anointed the feet of Jesus with an expensive perfume and then wiped his feet with her hair *(Luke 7:36 - 50)*.

Lacking modern medications or ointments of our time for healing wounds, infections and other skin conditions, herbs and spices mixed with olive oil were regularly applied for medicinal purposes. This was so customary that when Jesus sent the disciples out, two by two, they anointed many sick people, healing them, even though Jesus' instructions before he sent them out contained no reference to anointing *(Matt. 10:15-16)*. James, on the other hand, makes anointing with oil explicit in his instruction to elders summoned to pray for the sick *(James 5:14)*.

Anointing with olive oil had historical significance to the Jews. In the first Scriptural account of the use of olive oil in an act of consecration, Jacob anointed the rock he used as a pillow on the night, when in a dream, he observed angels ascending and descending upon a stairway that stretched from earth to heaven. That upended, anointed rock became a monument marking the location which Jacob then named Beth-El, the House of God *(Gen. 28:18-19)*.

Aaron and his sons were the first of a long line of priests who were anointed, consecrated and sanctified to minister to God as priests *(Ex. 28:41)* in the Tabernacle. In a Psalm, sung by the Israelites as they ascended to the Temple at Passover, David equates "dwelling together in unity" as being "like the precious oil upon the head, running down the beard of Aaron, down his garments upon the mountains of Zion" *(Psalm 133:1-2)*. Today, many Christian denominations, when they ordain or set apart men and women for ministry, anoint them with oil.

Prophets were also anointed *(1 Kings 19:16; 1 Chronicles. 16:22; Ps. 105:15)*. Anointing a king was equivalent to crowning him *(2 Sam. 2:4)*. The prophet Samuel anointed both Saul and David for kingship. David's anointing endured the test of time.

Exodus 30:24-25 contains the Lord's direction on exactly how the sacred oil for anointing various instruments of the Temple must be prepared, while Exodus 30:32-33 expressly prohibits oil of this mixture from being used to anoint the flesh of any person but a priest. Anyone who does "must be cut off from his people". This is why *Oil of Gladness* uses other biblically based and scripturally sound mixtures.

Even weapons of war were "anointed." The expression, "anoint the shield" *(Isa. 21:5)*, refers to the custom of rubbing oil on the leather of the shield so as to make it supple and fit for use in war.

Methods for burying the dead in New Testament times varied little from those described in the Old Testament. Specific and elaborate details had to be followed. First, the body was washed and anointed with oil. With limbs bound and face covered with a napkin, it was then wrapped (rolled) in linen along with great quantities of myrrh and aloes - embalming spices. Once prepared, the remains were temporarily placed on a niche in a family tomb to decay for a period of years. After this, the bones were removed and stacked into a small stone case, called an ossuary, so that the tomb might be reused.

It was these duties that summoned the women to Jesus' empty tomb that first Resurrection Morning *(Mark 16:1)*.

Anointing with Oil in Scripture

2

Scripture tells us that anointing with oil was a common practice. It accompanied many and varied occasions: beginning with Jacob's anointing of an upended rock he used as a pillow the night he saw angels ascending and descending from heaven upon a ladder *(Genesis 28:18 - 19)* to John's declarations that believers have an anointing from the "Holy One."

"But you have an anointing from the Holy One, and all of you know the truth" *(I John 2:20)*.

Psalm 133 describes the anointing of Aaron. Sacred anointing oil was poured over his head in such quantity that it ran down his beard and trickled down upon his robes, as if "the dew of Hermon were falling on Mount Zion". That would have taken a lot of anointing oil!

Even our Lord Jesus was well acquainted with the use of anointing oil. Recording the achievements of the sent out disciples, Mark's Gospel notes, "They went out and preached that people should repent. They drove out many demons and anointed many sick people with oil and healed them" *(Mark 6:12 - 13)*.

There were multiple purposes for anointing oil. It was a sign of consecration or act of setting apart someone or something for a holy or sacred use; as an act of hospitality to honor guests; as an ointment for medicinal purposes. Shields were anointed to keep them supple; bodies wrapped with anointed linen to reduce the stench of decay. Jesus was anointed in heaven and on earth to identify him as the "Anointed One."

Blind eyes received sight when "anointed" with a mixture of soil and spittle. The sick were healed when anointed. Timothy was consecrated for ministry when anointed. The Holy Spirit was poured out, as an anointing, when Jews and gentiles received Christ.

However one of the greatest encouragements in the use of anointing oil is given by James in his epistle –

> "Is anyone among you sick? Let him call for the elders of the church, and let them pray over him, anointing him with oil in the name of the Lord. And the prayer of faith will save the sick, and the Lord will raise him up. And if he has committed sins, he will be forgiven" *(James 5:14-15)*.

The Greek word used here for elder is 'presbuteros' and can refer not only to a rank in the church but to those mature in the faith.

There are two prerequisites described here for the use of anointing oil. Firstly, that the prayer is offered in the 'Name of The Lord' – Jesus, using the authority we have been given by Him to invoke His power, as in Acts 3:6 and Acts 16:18. Secondly, that the prayer is a 'prayer of faith' – bold confidence in our Lord Jesus *(Luke 17:6)*.

Therefore James provides a very practical mandate for one of the uses of anointing oil today.

Scripture gives us some insight into how anointing oil might be applied today.

- 🌿 As an act of consecration - to set someone or something apart for a special purpose in God's kingdom.

- 🌿 As an anointing upon their wives and children for protection, peace, blessing, by the spiritual leaders of the household as did the fathers of old.

- 🌿 In preparation for bible study, devotional time, fasting, praise and worship.

- 🌿 In response to an illness, a disease or a life threatening condition.

- 🌿 When coming against fear, anxiety or any other oppression of the enemy.

- ❧ As an accompaniment to baptism or rededication of someone's life.
- ❧ When invoking the Holy Spirit's involvement in someone's life.
- ❧ As the Holy Spirit leads - which can occur in any number of ways.

Today, a small amount of oil is customarily placed upon one or more fingers and then touched to or "rubbed" upon the forehead, top of the head, or affected body part of the person receiving prayer. Some use only one finger, dipped in oil to make the sign of the Cross upon the person's forehead while saying, "I anoint you in the name of the Father, the Son and the Holy Spirit/Ghost for…"

Words Spoken -

The words spoken are not specified in scripture, either.

They may range from simply saying:

- ❧ "May God bless you and keep you from all spiritual harm"
- ❧ "May God bless you and may the Holy Spirit bestow His abundant gifts upon you."

❧ "May God bless this marriage/home and fill it with love, understanding and patience."

❧ "May God bless you and may the blood of Jesus Christ protect you."

❧ "May God heal you and restore you to perfect health."

To more formal and prescribed:

"God, our redeemer, giver of heath and salvation, we give you thanks for this gift of oil. As the apostle anointed many who were sick, and you healed them, so may your Holy Spirit come on us and on this oil, that those who receive this anointing in repentance and faith may be made well in accordance with your will; through Jesus Christ our Savior. Amen" [1]

Or you may pray and bless the person as the Holy Spirit gives you the words (speak prophetically over the person).

Some practical considerations:

Always be sensitive to the person being prayed for.

Ask permission before anointing anyone with oil. Refusals are rare. When refusals come they are more likely due to some conflicting spiritual influence.

Some people are allergic to perfume. Because so many people have allergies, perfumes included, propriety calls us to ask individuals if they are allergic to oils or perfumes before indiscriminately anointing them.

Anointing oil may not wash off some materials.

Be careful not to get anointing oil on clothing, yours or the person you are anointing, that you do not ruin it.

This can be tricky, especially since there is mandate to lay hands on the person for whom you are praying. Keep a box of tissue or a cloth handkerchief handy to wipe off your hand.

Anointing need not be limited to an individual

Scripture demonstrates that anointing need not be limited to individuals. A home, business or church facility may be blessed or consecrated to the Lord in an anointing service.

With this intent, words like these may be spoken:

- 🌱 "May the Lord bless this house and all who live here."
- 🌱 "May the Holy Spirit bless and use this church for the work of the Kingdom."

🎵 "May the Lord protect all who dwell in the house."

🎵 "We bless this altar and consecrate it to Your service, Lord."

A Holy Exercise

Anointing with oil is a Holy exercise. It should not be performed indiscriminately. It must be done in order, according to the tenets of the Church to which you belong.

The most appropriate rule to follow, as to whether or not to anoint, would be the same rule governing every aspect of Christian life - wait upon the Lord and the Holy Spirit to direct you.

"But the Counselor, the Holy Spirit, whom the Father will send in my name, will teach you all things and will remind you of everything I have said to you" *(John 14:26)*.

"But when he, the Spirit of truth, comes, he will guide you into all truth. He will not speak on his own; he will speak only what he hears, and he will tell you what is yet to come. He will bring glory to me by taking from what is mine and making it known to you. All that belongs to the Father is mine. That is why I said the Spirit will take from what is mine and make it known to you" *(John 16:12 - 15)*.

It's the anointing that breaks the yoke.

(Isaiah 10:27)

"Leave her alone.
Why are you bothering her?"

Silly, impetuous Mary had done it again. She had crossed another line. Now she hadn't wasted just time, she had squandered a considerable amount of expensive perfume.

Six days before the Passover Feast, the festival for which nearly the entire Jewish population of Judea was gathered, she had unobtrusively slipped behind the reclining Jesus, a tightly gripped alabaster flask in her hand. Then, in front of her brother, the disciples and who knows how many others, she broke it open and poured its costly contents - a full ounce of spikenard - upon his head.

If any of those present failed to notice her impetuous behavior, the fragrance of the expensive perfume as it filled the entire house should have alerted them. Something significant had happened.

Indignant, the disciples, her sister Martha most likely included, chastised her. But Jesus restrained them.

"She has done a beautiful thing to me," Jesus declared. "The poor you will always have with you, and you can help them any time you want. But you will not always have me. She did what she could. She poured perfume on my body beforehand to prepare for my burial" *(Matthew 26:10 - 12; Mark 14:6 -8; John 12:7 - 8)*.

Poor Mary, how might her misguided act have offended them more! Focused upon Jesus ' rebuke, the disciples missed an additional reference to his death. If Judas had even the slightest bit of uncertainty left about ending his relationship with Jesus, it vanished right then. That very night, set on his path of betrayal, he sought out the chief priests and the others who were already planning to kill Jesus, and Lazarus as well *(Matthew 26:14; Mark 14:10; Luke 22:4; John 12:10)*.

If we were ever to identify any manner by which we might honor someone, what would better qualify than Mary's lavish gift? For, as Jesus prophesied, "I tell you the truth, wherever the gospel is preached throughout the world, what she has done will also be told, in memory of her" *(Matthew 26:13; Mark 14:9)*.

Only one Gospel, the one written by the gentile historian, neglects this event. Instead, in keeping with his readiness to uplift all women, Luke identifies another time, at the beginning of Jesus' ministry, when a woman of the street anointed Jesus in an identical manner *(Luke 7:36 - 38).*

Jesus, invited to dinner by Simon, one of the Pharisees, was eating when a woman, who had lived a sinful life, worked her way to where he was reclining. Kneeling behind him, weeping, she wet his feet with her tears, wiped them dry with her hair. After she had done this, she broke open her alabaster flask and anointed his feet.

"If this man were a prophet," Simon muttered to himself, "he would know who is touching him and what kind of woman she is - that she is a sinner."

"Simon, I have something to tell you." .

"Tell me, teacher."

Jesus recited the account of two men who owed different sums of money to a money-lender. One owed five hundred denarii, a great sum. The other owed him only fifty. No matter, neither of them could pay. So, for some unexplained reason, the moneylender canceled both of their debts.

"Now which of them loved him more?" Jesus asked his host.

Simon replied, "I suppose the one who had the bigger debt canceled."

"You have judged correctly," Jesus said.

Indicating the woman, Jesus went on.

"Do you see this woman?"

Simon nodded.

"I came into your house. You did not give me any water for my feet, but she wet my feet with her tears and wiped them with her hair. You did not give me a kiss, but this woman, from the time I entered, has not stopped kissing my feet. You did not put oil on my head, but she has poured perfume on my feet. Therefore, I tell you, her many sins have been forgiven, for she loved much. But he who has been forgiven little loves little."

Then Jesus said to her, "Your sins are forgiven. Your faith has saved you; go in peace."

The other guests murmured among themselves, "Who is this who even forgives sins?"

Both of these women drew harsh criticism for what they did. In each case, Jesus shushed their critics; the Pharisee, who had neglected to provide anointing oil when he entered his home and who chastised a woman of the street who did, a room full of scoffers who objected to the extravagant waste when the sister of a dear friend so impetuously offered it.

Public displays of affection like theirs still draw controversy. "Too emotional, too over the top," many would say. "Imagine! Humbling yourself to the point of weeping tears upon someone's feet and then drying them with your hair. Not on your life!" others might declare. If so, why did Jesus come so adamantly to the defense of the two women who were so far "out there" when they anointed him?

Perhaps the answer lies in Jesus' own words, "...for she loved much. But he who has been forgiven little loves little."

It might also be found in the words He spoke at another time - words also expressed by others, elsewhere in Scripture.

"Love the Lord your God with all your heart and with all your soul and with all your mind. This is the first and greatest commandment. And the second is like it: 'Love your neighbor as yourself.' All the Law and the Prophets hang on these two commandments."

By what they did, those women demonstrated a level of genuine, heartfelt love for Jesus that, when openly expressed, troubles others who have never known it. Why?

They have not experienced that love and forgiveness for themselves. Anointing someone with oil is one way of offering that experience.

"Be imitators of God, therefore, as dearly loved children and live a life of love, just as Christ loved us and gave himself up for us as a fragrant offering and sacrifice to God *(Ephesians 5:1, 2)*.

Frankincense

Both Frankincense (Boswellia) & Myrrh (Commiphora myrrha) are resins produced by certain trees that grow on both sides of the Red Sea.

"A tabernacle was set up. In its first room were the lamp stand, the table and the consecrated bread; this was called the Holy Place. Behind the second curtain was a room called the Most Holy Place, which had the golden altar of incense and the gold-covered ark of the covenant" *(Hebrews 9:2 - 3)*.

The incense that burned on the "golden altar of incense" in the "Most Holy Place" was composed of a blend of pure frankincense and fragrant spices identified by the LORD to Moses. Like the sacred anointing oil used solely to set apart the instruments within the temple and to consecrate the priests *(Exodus 30:22 - 26)*, strict restrictions governed its usage as well.

Whoever makes any like it to enjoy its fragrance must be cut off from his people" *(Exodus 30: 38)*.

Frankincense had a number of religious connotations.

Religious fervor - "My name will be great among the nations, from the rising to the setting of the sun. In every place incense and pure offerings will be brought to my name, because my name will be great among the nations," says the LORD Almighty *(Mal. 1:11)*.

Prayer - "…May my prayer be set before you like incense; may the lifting up of my hands be like the evening sacrifice" *(Psalm 141:1 - 2)*.

The prayers of the saints - "…The four living creatures and the twenty-four elders fell down before the Lamb. Each one had a harp and they were holding golden bowls full of incense, which are the prayers of the saints" *(Rev. 5:8; 8:3, 4)*.

The prayers that, one day, an angel of God will hurl down with fire upon the earth - "Then the angel took the censer, filled it with fire from the altar, and hurled it on the earth; and there came peals of thunder, rumblings, flashes of lightning and an earthquake" *(Rev. 8:5)*.

The gift, presented to Christ by the Magi, symbolizing his priestly office. "When they saw the star, they were overjoyed. On coming to the house, they saw the child with his mother Mary, and they bowed down and worshiped him. Then they opened their treasures and presented him with gifts of gold and of incense and of myrrh" *(Mt. 2:10 -11)*.

Myrrh

Myrrh, (Commiphora myrrha) a bitter and costly perfume was produced from the sticky white liquid harvested through incisions in the bark of a tree which grew in Africa, Arabia, and Ethiopia. It is mentioned in Scripture as being one of the most valuable of items *(Gen. 43:11)* and constituted a principal ingredient of the holy anointing oil *(Ex. 30:23)*.

At Christ's anointing, myrrh scented his robes *(Psalm 45:6 - 9)*. At his birth myrrh was given by wise men from the east as a gift for one who was to die *(Matt. 2:9-12)*. At his crucifixion myrrh was offered to ease His pain *(Mark 15:23)*. At his tomb myrrh with aloes and strips of linen wrapped his body *(John 19:39)*.

Of the letters to the Seven Churches in Revelation the church at Smyrna, which means "Myrrh", was one church against which the Lord held nothing.

"These are the words of him who is the First and the Last, who died and came to life again. I know your afflictions and your poverty yet you are rich! I know the slander of those who say they are Jews and are not, but are a synagogue of Satan. Do not be afraid of what you are about to suffer. I tell you, the devil will put some of you in prison to test you, and you will suffer persecution for ten days. Be

faithful, even to the point of death, and I will give you the crown of life"
(Rev. 2:8 – 10).

30   Might myrrh provide an appropriate fragrance for those being persecuted - for those who suffer affliction, poverty, and slander?

Rose of Sharon

While we are uncertain of the modern translation of "Rose of Sharon", many scholars agree it is most likely the Cistus, or rock-rose commonly found in the Mount Carmel area of Palestine. Jesus is often called the "Rose of Sharon" because of the beauty and sweetness His presence brings.

"I am a rose of Sharon, a lily of the valleys" (Solomon 2:1).

Known for its beauty and fragrance and mentioned only twice in Scripture, it grew in great abundance throughout the entire fertile, coastal region of Israel, from Caesarea to Joppa, where vast groves of oranges now flourish.

Called "the Rose of Sharon" by King Solomon, it is one of the names of Christ from which we learn something about his personality. Unlike "the Bright and Morning Star," distant and far off, the roses of Sharon grew where anyone could admire their beauty and enjoy their fragrance. The "Son of the Most High God" is not only beautiful and fragrant, he is also accessible to all who seek him.

Identified simply as a "crocus" by Isaiah *(35:1)*, we learn even more about our Savior.

"The desert and the parched land will be glad; the wilderness will rejoice and blossom. Like the crocus, it will burst into bloom; it will rejoice greatly and shout for joy. The glory of Lebanon will be given to it, the splendor of Carmel and Sharon; they will see the glory of the LORD, the splendor of our God" *(Isaiah 35:2)*.

What more appropriate fragrance, for times of rejoicing and great joy, might there be than the sweet smelling "Rose of Sharon"?

Lily of the Valley

The term "lily" covered a wide variety of flowers ranging from colorful to the purest of white. It is probably the latter to which Jesus refers when He told us, "And why do you worry about clothes? See how the lilies of the field grow.

They do not labor or spin. Yet I tell you that not even Solomon in all his splendor was dressed like one of these" *(Matthew 6:28 - 29; Luke 12:27 - 28)*.

Known for their whiteness and beauty, "Lily of the Valley" carpeted all of the low places of Israel. In contrast to their harsh surroundings, Jesus saw them as being even more beautiful than the jewel bedecked robes of King Solomon.

In sweetness and purity they bloom amidst thorns and briars. In them, those who are wounded see Christ as vulnerably exposed and experiencing the same sufferings and humiliations as themselves. When crushed, their petals give off a sweet fragrance akin to the aroma of Christ amongst those being saved, even the fragrance of life itself *(2 Cor. 2:15 - 16)*.

Representative of the purity of the Savior, "Lily of the Valley" symbolizes the freedom destined for all who come to know him as their sovereign LORD.

Use of this fragrance would seem appropriate for all who come before the Lord to repent of their sin, surrender their lives and receive Christ as Savior. Might it also be suitable for those recommitting their lives to Him? Its pure fragrance would certainly qualify it for anyone seeking a refreshing touch from Christ Jesus, the Anointed One.

Oil of Gladness – Unscented Olive Oil

"…to comfort all who mourn, and provide for those who grieve in Zion— to bestow on them a crown of beauty instead of ashes, the oil of gladness instead of mourning, and a garment of praise instead of a spirit of despair.

They will be called oaks of righteousness, a planting of the LORD for the display of his splendor" *(Isaiah 61:3)*.

The "sting of death" was very real to the Jews of Jesus' day. Mandatory days of personal and ritualistic mourning followed the passing of every loved one. On the cross Jesus carried the sting of death in our place. By this he cancelled the need for many of those rituals.

Silence regarding the composition of this "oil of gladness," various other scriptures suggest that whenever "anointing with oil" is mentioned, that oil is "elaion," the pure, unscented "golden oil" extracted by beating, pressing, and crushing the fruit of the olive tree. This "golden oil" fueled the lamp stands which remained lit day and night in the Temple. Symbolic of the precious blood of Christ, it was poured out for our salvation upon the Cross of Calvary [2].

Now, in place of sprinkled ashes upon the heads of mourners, Christ bestows a crown. Instead of mourning, he blesses and comforts with soothing oil. For a spirit of despair and rented garments of goat hair, he calls for robes of praise. Rather than pain and weakness, he envisions the stalwart oak of righteousness.

"Where, O death, is your victory? Where, O death, is your sting?" *(Hosea 13:14; I Cor, 15:55)*.

You are swallowed up in victory *(I Cor. 15:54)*. The old order of things has passed away, for he who sits on the throne "is making all things new". A day is coming when every tear will be wiped away - when death, mourning, tears and pain will be no more. Are not these words trustworthy and true? *(Rev. 21:4 - 5)*.

When blessing those in need of comfort, those who mourn or when declaring renewal over others at "new beginnings," might not this unscented "Oil of Gladness" qualify?

Latter Rain

"Be patient, then, brothers, until the Lord's coming. See how the farmer waits for the land to yield its valuable crop and how patient he is for the autumn and spring rains" *(James 5:7)*.

The term "Latter Rain" as it is used by James has little to do with weather. He uses it as an illustration of the need for patience during dark times - the patience of the farmer who waits through bleak winter months for the "latter" rains that come in time to swell the grain just prior to the Spring harvest.

This is James' way of encouraging those who struggle through painful circumstances, enduring uncertainty and troubled relationships, patiently to stand firm. He goes on to warn against grumbling at each other because of the judgment it brings. He assures us that "the Lord is near," and alerts that "the Judge is standing at the door!" Directing our attention to the day when the Lord returns, he reminds us of the promise that all trouble and suffering will pass away *(Rev. 21:3 - 5)*.

What a great and glorious day that will be! But, until that day arrives, we must encourage each other, pray without ceasing, and look to the hope that we have in Christ Jesus.

Use of this fragrance might offer hope, encouragement and incentive to someone needing to stand firm as he or she eagerly awaits the fulfillment of all of the promises of God.

Spikenard

An extract of the root of a plant that grew in the Himalayas, (Nardostachys jatamansi) the perfume it produced constituted one of the most precious and expensive imports of Roman Palestine. Its name, "the Indian spike", came from its appearance - many hairy spikes extending out from one root.

The fragrance of this spice filled the room the evening Mary, the sister of Lazarus, broke open an alabaster jar and lovingly poured its contents over Jesus' head *(John 12:3)*. "When she poured this perfume on my body, she did it to prepare me for burial. I tell you the truth, wherever this gospel is preached throughout the world, what she has done will also be told, in memory of her" *(Matt. 26:12 - 13)*.

True to this prophecy, Matthew, Mark and John, each mention Mary's extravagant gift. Luke points to an earlier event, when a woman of the street, "stood behind him at his feet weeping". This sinful woman then wet his feet with her tears, wiped them with her hair, kissed them and poured the identical fragrance upon them *(Luke 7:38)*. Her action, too, drew protest.

"You did not give me a kiss, but this woman, from the time I entered, has not stopped kissing my feet. You did not put oil on my head, but she has poured perfume on my feet. Therefore, I tell you, her many sins have been forgiven, for she loved much. But he who has been forgiven little loves little" *(Luke 7:47)*.

As an act of love, praise and worship, in response to forgiveness or in preparation for Eternal Life, this fragrance might once again fill the "house" wherever the Gospel is proclaimed.

Pomegranate

From the Latin, pomum ("apple") and granatus ("seeded"), or "apple of many seeds." From the Greek, panspermia, "all seed."

Did you know when those of the Jewish faith celebrate Rosh HaShanna in the latter weeks of September, many of them make it a point to include pomegranates with their feasts? Why would they do that? Because they like us have learned of the many healthy properties of this "apple with many seeds"? No, because their tradition portrays the pomegranate as a symbol of righteousness.

Jewish tradition teaches that the pomegranate has a total of 613 seeds (even though they admit that the actual number may vary with each fruit). This number corresponds with the 613 mitzvot or commandments contained in the Torah. As the two days of Rosh Hashanna approach, the shofar is blown each morning to warn the people to, "Repent, now! Don't wait until after 'Rosh HaShanah,' the "birthday of Creation."

In the time of Solomon's Temple, there were two free standing pillars of bronze, each twenty-seven feet tall. Engraved above a band of chains on the top portion of each pillar interlaced with a lattice work of seven chains, were two rows of 100 pomegranates each. These pillars stood on either side of the eastern entrance of the temple; the one on the left was named Jakin ("he establishes"), and the one on the right, Boaz ("in Him is strength"). The two pillars were there as a reminder that the Lord had "established His house" and the "He would maintain it forever." (I Kings 7:20; 7:42);

Had you lived in an earlier time, you would have been aware of another fact. The first reference to pomegranates appeared in God's instructions on how Aaron's priestly robe should be hemmed.

"Make pomegranates of blue, purple and scarlet yarn around the hem of the robe, with gold bells between them." Exodus 28:33

Clothed in priestly finery and adorned with the symbols of his authority, Aaron would have jingled with the sound of many golden bells as he walked in the temple (Sirach 45:8–9). Spaced evenly between the bells would have been pomegranates woven of blue, purple and scarlet yarn. Those living at that time would not have known that the ringing golden bells would come to symbolize the Gifts of the Holy Spirit.

Nor would they have heard the speculation that the multi-colored yarn pomegranates would come to symbolize the Fruits of the Spirit.

"But the fruit of the Spirit is love, joy, peace, long suffering, gentleness, goodness, faith, meekness, temperance: against such there is no law." Galatians 5:22-23

Reading the Song of Solomon, either then or now, you would learn that there is another prophetic symbolism for the pomegranate - the Spirit of love, the kind of love only experienced by those immersed in the fullness of God's forgiveness as it is demonstrated in Christ Jesus.

In the lyrics of the Song of Songs, the "apple of many seeds" is also associated with beauty (Song of Songs 4:3), with luxury (Song of Songs 8:2), with the timing for when love is given –

"Let us go early into the vineyards; Let us see if the vine has flowered, If its blossoms have opened, If the pomegranates are in bloom. There I will give my love to you."

Song of Songs 7:13.

The fruit is even found within a beautiful garden (Song of Songs 7:13) and within a vision of the Church - as being an "orchard of pomegranates" (Song of Songs 4:13).

In other places, this luscious fruit is associated with the abundance of the Promised Land (Deut. 8:8; Numbers 13:13).

In the early days of Jesus' ministry, a woman of the street entered, uninvited, into a house where Jesus was a dinner guest. Kneeling at his feet, she anointed them. With her tears, she dampened them. With her hair, she dried them. With her lips, she continually kissed them. When the host, a Pharisee, challenged Jesus for allowing this, he responded with the teaching of the "Unforgiving Debtor." When he had finished his teaching he asked, "Do you see this woman?" He then went on to declare, "Her sins, which are many, have been forgiven, for she loved much; but he who is forgiven little loves little." (Luke 7:41-48)

Have you heard that many Jewish scholars hold that the "forbidden fruit" offered by Eve to Adam in the Garden was not an apple but, instead, "an apple of many seeds" – a pomegranate? If their speculation is accurate, might it suggest that Adam's partaking of the "apple of 613 seeds" symbolizes more than disobedience to just the one command…

"But of the fruit of the tree which is in the midst of the garden, God hath said, Ye shall not eat of it, neither shall ye touch it, lest ye die." Genesis 3:3

Might it also suggest that Adam would be in disobedience of all

613 commandments? Perhaps it would be safer and less threatening to stick with the apple theory.

Henry, Matthew, Matthew Henry's Commentary on the Bible, *41* (Peabody, MA: Hendrickson Publishers) 1997

6

Anointing Oil has a very long history in both ancient and Biblical cultures. Its use has varied widely but with one common dominator – the benefit of the recipient. Sometimes this would have been limited to the physical – cleansing, refreshing, renewing. However most often there was a powerful spiritual benefit as well: healing, consecration deliverance, as clearly recorded for us in the Bible, both in the Old & New Testaments.

There is nothing 'magical' about the oil itself. It is always the power of the living God at work amongst His people that provides the desired result. The oil simply provides the symbolic picture of the interaction being requested.

We believe today, in the Twenty-First century, that anointing with oil still has great spiritual benefit. Testimonies abound of the way the Lord has answered prayers and moved in power upon a request. (The cry of the heart following anointing with oil.) We pray you will witness the wonderful miraculous power of our risen Lord.

Should you have questions, require further information or would like to share your story, please, contact us via the internet at www.everygoodgift.com. We would be delighted to hear from you. It is our joy and privilege to serve the Kingdom of God by providing you with this powerful aid to prayer and ministry.

Bill Edmunds

Bill Edmunds lives with his wife Joan in Clearlake, California where they are the directors of the Healing Rooms of Lake County, an affiliate of the International Association of Healing Rooms, Spokane, Washington. They worship at the Cobb Mountain Community Fellowship in nearby Cobb, California.

Bill is a retired police command officer and now enjoys his retirement from full time police work. As a part time instructor for Behavior Analysis Training Institute, he continues to train police investigators in the both basic and advanced interview and interrogation techniques.

Desiring to better understand the biblical practice of anointing with oil, he conducted an extensive study of the scriptures in order to determine its place in our Christian faith. In a study of the names of Jesus, as they relate to the fragrances of various anointing oils, he developed the information contained in this book. He has been a long term friend of *Every Good Gift* and uses our anointing oils regularly.

See his book, All Roads Lead to Zion, available through Paracletus Publishing at www.paracletus.com

After making my first purchase of *Oil of Gladness* anointing oil, several years ago, I regretted not purchasing one of the oil holders at the same time. I looked for them another time without success. Using the 800 phone number provided on the bottle, I ordered one from *Oil of Gladness* directly. That's when I first heard Michelle Zwicky's testimony regarding the early beginnings of *Oil of Gladness*. Only a Berean tug at my spirit kept me from using *Oil of Gladness* anointing oils right then. I needed to know that anointing was for today and that scented anointing oils were appropriate to use. I turned to Scripture for the answer.

After many hours of study and research, much of which makes up the content of this publication, I determined not only was anointing for today, but each one of the fragrances offered by *Oil of Gladness* had a rich biblical history and application. Today when the Holy Spirit directs me to anoint someone for healing or any other purpose, I am not only able to cite the Biblical authority for doing it, I can give a witness about the *Oil of Gladness* fragrance used.

Would God approve of that? Based upon my own experiences I would say He would - and does.

Wm. I. "Bill" Edmunds

Appendix

[1] United Church of Christ, The Committee on Healing

Ministries (U.C.C. Book of Worship)

[2] Henry, Matthew, Matthew Henry's Commentary on the Bible, (Peabody, MA: Hendrickson Publishers) 1997.

30 Day Devotional

by Pastor C. Neil Sayers

Drawing Insight & Inspiration from Biblical events

surrounding the use of Anointing Oil.

Each devotional concludes with an opportunity

for personal response and journaling:

🌿 A Song to Sing – Verses from the Psalms to lift your spirit.

🌿 A Promise to Pursue – Scriptures to bring strength & hope.

🌿 A Prayer to Pray – Words of praise and petition.

🌿 Journal jottings – Space for your response in your own words.

Precious Peace

Mark 14:3-9

This beautiful incident in the life of Jesus has inspired theologians & preachers, poets and artists, throughout the preceding generations. Well of course it would; Jesus Himself prophesied the fact in Mark 14:9.

Yet in the countless retelling of this story some of its relevance for us today is in danger of being lost.

As we begin our devotional journey together, let us start by reflecting again upon this both precious and powerful event.

Consider firstly the context of the story. Jesus' earthly ministry is drawing toward its dramatic conclusion. Judas Iscariot so upset by this seemingly wasteful act goes immediately to the Chief Priest to arrange betrayal (Mark 14:10). Darkness is closing in, evil forces are gathering. Yet in the midst of that here is a story of extravagant love that stands out like a glistening diamond.

That's what happens when we pour our love and adoration upon the "light of the world". There is a peace and presence which can claim the most troubled of hearts in the darkness of hours.

Perhaps you feel very much in the midst of a dark time; forces seem to be gathering against you. His invitation is, "Sit with Me, engage with Me. Let My love bring light into your life and quiet your heart, know My precious peace, My beloved child."

As the song says "When we gaze into His loveliness all the things that surround me became shadows in the light of Him."

A Song to Sing: Psalm 18:6

A Promise to Pursue: John 14:27

A Prayer to Pray: Precious Lord Jesus, You are the Prince of Peace, and I look to You now to bring me peace; quiet my heart and spirit. Let Your light shine in to me and out through me.

In Jesus Name, Amen.

Journal jottings:

Pursuing Purity
Mark 14:3-9

Isn't it interesting how one event can be viewed in two very different ways? How a single historical happening can be interpreted so differently but those who observed the event?

For example a Superbowl will be viewed very different by the fans of each team. And any police officer will tell you that taking witness statements of a traffic accident can be quite a challenge often their views of the event can be very varied.

So it was with the incident we are currently focusing upon. For Jesus, Mary's act was an expression of extravagant love. However for much of the witnessing group of people, especially Judas, it was a preposterous waste.

Yet, upon closer examination we can see the Judas' reaction was not just on a physical level but also on a spiritual level. Jesus says in verse 6 (NIV) that 'she has done a beautiful thing', and in The Message - 'wonderfully significant'

The Greek word used here is 'kalos' – meaning beautiful by reason of purity, of heart and life, therefore making it a praiseworthy & noble act.

The purity of her motive – worshipful love and adoration was what Jesus was moved by. Judas too! What was perhaps his motive for following Jesus -acclaim, power, victory over Roman oppressors, financial gain? We cannot be certain. However for someone to betray his friend so quickly reveals a motive far from pure. In direct contrast to Mary. Perhaps in Judas' response we hear guilt too?

The Lord Jesus always sees our heart, our motive. We must examine our own hearts continually; we can become so corrupted by the world – where love is often given for gain. Jesus calls for a love that gives. Our model is His own expression of love – these words describe it well - sacrificially, understandingly, forgivingly, and unconditionally. Do they describe our love for Him and those around us? The one who examines our hearts knows.

A Song to Sing: Psalm 24:3-5

A Promise to Pursue: Matthew 5:8

A Prayer to Pray: Lord Jesus, examine my heart, my desire is to walk with You in purity. My cry aligns with the Apostle Paul – that I will be 'filled with love that comes from a pure heart.'

In Jesus Name Amen

Journal jottings:

Pleasing Passion
Mark 14:3-9

Have you ever given consideration to the way growing numbers of words in our English language have been 'adjusted' in their meaning over recent years? For example –

Cool was a measure of temperature. Sweet was a description of a taste experience. Awesome was only ever placed in the same sentence as God or Lord.

Passion too, is a word of which much of it true meaning has been misused in modern times. As it relates to our story it provides an accurate description of Mary's love for her Lord – 'an exhibition of fondness & feeling.' Nothing was held back. Perfume, probably a family heirloom used in its entirety to show affection & worship.

Would you describe yourself as a passionate person? Maybe you're passionate about your favorite sports team, your former college, or fondest pastime. Now of course there is nothing wrong with that. Providing the preeminent passion of your life is Jesus.

In fact one of the strongest statements ever made by Jesus as recorded in the scriptures is found in Revelation 3:16. Permit me to paraphrase – Jesus says - I see right through you. You're insipid. Cold hearts I can work with. On fire followers I like. But half hearted, fair weather Christians - you make me sick.

Strong words, so that is why we should ask ourselves regularly – 'Where am I on His temperature scale today?'

A Song to Sing: Psalm 18:1-2

A Promise to Pursue: Psalm 31:16

A Prayer to Pray: Lord, please enable me to be more passionate about You and the things of Your kind. Keep me focused on what is really important today. Keep my heart in tune with You.

In Jesus Name Amen

Journal jottings:

Prophetic Proclamation

Mark 14:3-9

The final two verses of this beautiful story underscore the prophetic significance of Mary's act. A significance that Mary was almost certainly completely unaware of.

Yet her action proclaimed to the assembled people and as Jesus pointed out it touches you & I today. Right now as you read this page you fulfill the very words of Jesus. What a privilege.

Our love & worship too should be prophetic. Prophetic in the sense that we proclaim who Jesus is and what He has done. Our lives should reflect His grace, His love, and His joy.

As we live out our lives in our families, marriages, communities and workplaces do we reveal Jesus? Or do we get so caught up in the things of life we forget what and even more importantly who this is really all about.

During a recent visit to Sea World San Antonio, I watched with amusement as a Dad and his two daughters became distracted by something spotted in the flower bed on their way to see the Shamu show. "Oh Daddy look a slug, Daddy come look" the girls cried. "Yes but come along we going to miss the show" the Dad replied. The girls were insistent "But Daddy wait, come look a slippery, slimly slug." Exasperated, his reply was firm "Sweethearts, forget the slug. You are going to miss the main attraction - Shamu the killer whale!"

How often are we too sidelined by the little slugs of life that we are in danger of neglecting the main attraction – Jesus? Do we live life prophetically in such a way that it points to Jesus? Prophetic by word, action and deed. Perhaps today is the day to make that call, write that letter, visit that sick friend- pray for them, and anoint them.

A Song to Sing: Psalm 119:172-173

A Promise to Pursue: Romans 12:6-8

A Prayer to Pray: Lord Jesus, please help me live my life in such a way that I always reflect You. I yearn to be Your feet & hands reaching out to needy world. May my words be Your words - bringing hope & strength. In Jesus Name Amen

Journal jottings:

Possibilities Pursued

Mark 14:3-9

Do you sometimes feel you don't have much to offer? You observe others with talents and gifts being selected and used for Kingdom service, but no one comes to ask for your help.

Ever feel like the little child always left till last when the two Captains were picking the teams from among your class mates?

Maybe Mary felt that way? Her sister Martha always so busy using her ability for hospitality. Her brother Lazarus – well, talk about a testimony! "Oh yeah, I was rotting in the grave when Jesus resurrected me!" But Mary – what could she offer?

Perhaps the most encouraging words in this whole story are found in verse v8. Jesus says - She did what she could, when she could (The Message).

That is all Jesus ever requires of us. To do what we can with what we've got. Then He takes it and multiplies it beyond our wildest dreams.

Mary's act is proclaimed around the world. A little boy's lunch feeds hungry thousands. A loud mouth fisherman preaches and thousand are swept into the Kingdom. A promiscuous woman becomes the first missionary.

Ordinary people doing extraordinary things. People like you and me. When we come to the Prince of Peace in purity, love on Him with passion; He takes what we have, multiplies it and uses it to extend the kingdom. The possibilities are endless.

The old benediction puts it so well. Go forth into all the world with peace. Be of good courage. Hold fast to that which is good. Render to no man evil for evil. Strengthen the faint hearted. Support the weak. Help the afflicted. Honor all men. Love & serve the Lord rejoicing in the power of the Holy Spirit

A Song to Sing: Psalm 119:33-34

A Promise to Pursue: Isaiah 64:8

A Prayer to Pray: Loving Lord, I am Yours. Take what I have am and use it. Multiply it that I might serve You and help advance the Kingdom. I am ready, I am willing and You are able. In Jesus Name Amen

Journal jottings:

Marking the Moment

Genesis 28:10-22

In the most unlikely of places God shows up: Gideon about his daily chores at the winepress. Jonah in the belly of a whale. Isaiah praying in the Temple. Peter fishing. Nathanael having his quiet time under his favorite shade tree. A lame man begging as he's done for years. Paul on a journey to Damascus. And in our text, Jacob catching forty winks. Everyday routine activities, then suddenly – God!

Of course God is omnipresence. He is everywhere all of the time, but invisible most of the time. Yet on occasions like these He makes Himself known.

For us, too. We might be doing the laundry, commuting to work, or jogging in the park, when suddenly - God. He speaks to our heart, drops a word of revelation into our mind, brings a sense of His presence, touches our spirit. In the midst of the ordinary comes a meaningful moment with God.

Our response? Like Jacob we should mark the moment. Anoint it. Build a memorial, maybe not in the physical sense, but with a heart response. With praise and thanksgiving and a note in our Bible or journal. A conscious act so that we mark the moment making it easier to recall the next time we need a faith boost, a little encouragement.

Life is so busy we can quickly let the memory of such precious moments slip. We need to be creative and "anoint" these suddenly God moments.

A Song to Sing: Psalm 27:14

A Promise to Pursue: Deuteronomy 31:6

A Prayer to Pray: Lord Jesus, how I yearn for Your presence. Meet with me, reveal Yourself to me, speak to me. I, Your servant, am ready. In Your Name I ask this, Amen.

Journal jottings:

Rocky Roads
Genesis 28:10-22

In ancient times, a King had a
boulder placed on a roadway. Then
he hid himself and watched to see if
anyone would remove the huge rock. Some of the king's wealthiest
merchants and courtiers came by and simply walked around it. Many
loudly blamed the King for not keeping the roads clear, but none did
anything about getting the stone out of the way.

Then a peasant came along carrying a load of vegetables. Upon
approaching the boulder, the peasant laid down his burden and tried
to move the stone to the side of the road. After much pushing and
straining, he finally succeeded. He then noticed a purse lying in the
road where the boulder had been. The purse contained many gold coins
and a note from the King indicating that the gold was for the person

who removed the boulder from the roadway. The peasant learned what many of us have trouble understanding. Every obstacle presents an opportunity to improve our condition.

Rocks in the road. Life has many. Some we place there ourselves, some arrive through no fault of our own. Many though will have the potential of being used by the Lord to work His perfect will and way in us and through us. God can and God does.

So it was with Jacob. His rock became a pillow. Can you imagine? Yet the resulting night's sleep brought a powerful prophetic dream that revealed the Lord's plan for this man's life.

Beloved, facing some rocks in the road? Ask the Lord to use them to reveal Himself to you. After all that's the very essence of Romans 8:28 " And we know that God causes everything to work together for the good of those who love God and are called according to His purpose for them" (NLT).

A Song to Sing: Psalm 25:4-5

A Promise to Pursue: Philippians 4:13

A Prayer to Pray: My Lord, my Savior, my Friend, please pour upon me Your strength. Please give me Your peace that I might know your guiding way on the roads of life. In Jesus Name, Amen.

Journal jottings:

Sweet Dreams

Genesis 28:10-22

Our final reflection on the story has to do with dreams. Jacob's dream was an awe inspiring picture of heavenly beings descending and ascending from Heaven to Earth, of stairways and of the Lord Himself. It was a revelation of promises - of vast real estate, of millions of descendents, of protection and perpetual presence. Wow! Some dream!

Fascinating things, dreams. Did you know that on average we have two or more dreams a night, even though we may not recall them? Therefore that equates to over six years spent dreaming during our lifetime!

The Lord often speaks through dreams. In the Bible there are many recordings of the Lord speaking to his people through dreams. Joseph–son of Jacob and perhaps the most famous of all much to the frustration of his brothers, also Solomon, Nebuchadnezzar and of course Joseph husband of Mary to name but a few.

On the subject of dreams the prophet Joel reminds us in Joel 2:28 "....Your old men shall dream dreams , Your young men shall see visions." All too soon we seem to qualify for the former.

How often do you ask the Lord to give you a dream? To reveal Himself to you as you sleep?

Jacob anointed his "pillow" after his dream; perhaps we should consider anointing ours before we sleep.

Good night, God bless, sweet dreams.

A Song to Sing: Psalm 8:1

A Promise to Pursue: Psalm 3:5

A Prayer to Pray: Lord Jesus, Prince of Peace, grant me Your peace as I sleep, so that I might truly be renewed and refreshed to face another day. And if I dream, my cry is like that of Samuel – speak, Lord, for Your servant is listening. Amen and Amen.

Journal jottings:

The Anointing of Unity
Psalm 133

Oil in the hair, on a beard, running over clothes. At first glance it all seems a little bizarre. Defiantly very Old Testament. Rather messy, too. However over the course of the next few days let's take a second look and unwrap this image so that it will speak to us today in the 21st Century.

The context of this song (for which we sadly don't have the music) is no coincidence. It is the second to last of a section of songs called the "Songs of Ascent." sung by the people of Israel as they travelled up to Jerusalem to attend the festivals and feasts. Journeying from their towns, villages and rural areas, they sang these songs with joy and thanksgiving. Jesus himself would have sung these very words. We know from Luke's gospel he attended the gathering in Jerusalem (Luke 2:42)

What more appropriate message – brotherly love and unity – recounted as you travel with fellow believers toward a celebration of the God of love. Look around you next time you're in church. Those people are your family. You share a common blood line – the blood of Jesus. You're traveling with them on the journey called life.

Ask yourself, am I dwelling in unity with them? Is the oil of harmony flowing? If not, why not?

A Song to Sing: Psalm 5:7

A Promise to Pursue: John 13:34

A Prayer to Pray: Loving Lord, help me love the way You want me to. Touch my heart, touch my life that I might be the loving person I need to be. In Jesus Name, Amen.

Journal jottings:

10

Sitting not Standing
Psalm 133

The Hebrew word for "dwell" used in verse 1 literally means to sit down. Sitting down in unity with your fellow believers is a good, agreeable to the will of God, pleasing and precious thing.

Standing up speaks a very different message. "I'm standing up for myself." "Standing up for my rights." Me, myself, I. "I'tis"– the disease that's epidemic in our world. A disease that makes unity and harmony very difficult to achieve.

Now this may come as a surprise to you, but this disease is prevalent in our churches too. There is a church in the Holy land, shared by two congregations. It has an ugly old ladder leaning against the wall of its beautiful ornate sanctuary. It has been there for decades. No one can remember who put it there in the first place. Each congregation says the other is responsible for putting it away. And so the standoff remains; no flowing oil of harmony and unity in that church.

Reflect for a moment. Are there any ladders in your life? Anything that is an issue between you and your church family? Is there someone you should call, write, send an email, or sit down with?

Go ahead. The cure for "I'tis" is an oil. The anointed oil of loving unity. Pour some today.

A Song to Sing: Psalm 141:3

A Promise to Pursue: 1 John 2:3-6

A Prayer to Pray: Jesus, more of You and less of me, that is my earnest prayer. It's all about you, Lord. I'm here because of You. I'm here for You. Help me keep that fact in focus daily. In Your Name I pray, Amen.

Journal jottings:

Oil Pouring

Psalm 133

Oil—exquisitely fragrant, methodically prepared to a scriptural recipe, costly. Poured out upon a head, flowing down over a beard and overrunning to the very end of his garments.

Vivid imagery that tells us:

To flow so freely was a liberal pouring of oil. Nothing held back, extravagant and generous. (So unlike the modern way of just dabbing oil on the forehead!) It reminds us that our love for one another must be generous, freely given and without condition.

Love, so often presumed to be a feeling, an emotion, is more truly a choice. Love based on feeling may soon evaporate. Love that's a choice, a conscious decision, stands a much great chance of going the distance. "Love is blind"– not really. True love has its eyes wide open. Love that loves in spite of, not because of. That's why the oil is firstly poured upon the head. The choice to love must start there.

The beard was a sign of maturity, status and authority. The flowing oil of Christian love recognizes and respects those God has placed over us in positions of authority and responsibility.

To the hem of his garment, this flowing love permeates every facet of life. It should be real, practical and permanent.

Ask yourself this question. Am I pouring out love or withholding it? Am I in the flow or blocking it? Am I revealing it or resenting it?

A Song to Sing: Psalm 136:13

A Promise to Pursue: Romans 12:10-13

A Prayer to Pray: Lord, help me to love generously, even extravagantly. My I love the way You love, sacrificially, forgivingly, understandingly, unconditionally. In Jesus Name, Amen.

Journal jottings:

92

12

Dew Descending

Psalm 133

Have you ever walked across a lawn or field on a clear cool dewy morning? Ever felt the refreshing coolness of dew on your bare skin? Ever tasted it? Try it sometime.

In our song dew speaks of a cooling and refreshing life-giving liquid. Very necessary for life in the hot, dry lands of Israel. Harmony between believers is like such dew. It brings refreshing, sweet life in a dry barren world of malice, bitterness and sin.

Paul reminds us of the dew-like qualities of love in 1 Corinthians 13: 4-7, " Love is patient and kind. Love is not jealous or boastful or proud or rude. Love does not demand its own way. Love is not irritable, and it keeps no record of when it has been wronged. It is never glad about injustice but rejoices whenever the truth wins out. Love never gives up, never loses faith, is always hopeful, and endures through every circumstance"(NLT).

Read it through again, but this time replace the word "love" with your own name. Does it ring true? Does it sound right? Sometimes maybe, sometimes maybe not. Yet, with the Lord's help, when we strive to love our church family with that kind of love, then we'll feel the dew begin to settle on our relationships.

A Song to Sing: Psalm 121:2

A Promise to Pursue: Galatians 5:22

A Prayer to Pray: Loving Lord, my all those descriptions of love found in Paul's letter to the church in Corinth be true of my love. In Jesus Name, Amen.

Journal jottings:

13

Forgiveness Flowing – One
Psalm 133

Before we leave this song and its vivid imaginary of flowing oil and refreshing dew, let me make a very practical, vitally important practical application on the subject of love.

There is a word in the Bible. It is just a little word, tiny in fact, only two letters. Yet its significance is HUGE when it appears in the sentence given by Jesus in Matthew 6:12, "And forgive us our sins, just as we have forgiven those who have sinned against us"

(NLT). The little word – as.

Forgiveness is foundational for love, unity and harmony. Of course it's not easy! C. S. Lewis spoke for all of us when he said, "Forgiveness is a lovely idea until you have someone to forgive."

The problem is that forgiveness is much misunderstood. This is what forgiveness is not:

Condoning. Forgiving someone does not mean you approve of what they did.

Forgetting. Forgive and forget? If the offence is small yes, you will probably forget all about it. But if it is big, you may never forget even if you do forgive. But it's the recounting and relaying of it that is the problem. Forgiveness is not dependent on forgetting.

Denying. Been really hurt by someone? The pain may be so great that it's easier to deny it rather than deal with it. However this might lead to illness–spiritual, physical, mental.

Pretending. You may pretend it's all okay, try to brush it off, but deep inside you harbor resentment and bitterness. This, too, can lead to illness. Best deal with it openly.

Losing. The person who forgives is not a loser, but when forgiveness flows, winning healing is ministered.

Take some time to examine your own heart. Does it harbor any unforgiveness? Toward someone? Toward yourself even?

A Song to Sing: Psalm 85:2

A Promise to Pursue: Colossians 2:12

A Prayer to Pray: Lord Jesus, thank You for paying the price of my sins, once and for all. Thank You that I am now justified – just as if it never happened. Wonderful Savior, Thank You, Amen.

Journal jottings:

14

Forgiveness Flowing – Two

Psalm 133

Now let us reflect upon what forgiveness is:

Choosing, not feeling. You may not feel like forgiving, but it is a choice. It should not be based or whether you feel like it or not. The scripture is clear. Colossians 3:13, Forgive whatever grievances you may have against one another... Forgive as the Lord forgave you. Forgiveness is a command, a standard, a choice.

Choosing not to dwell on the hurt. Sometimes the memory of the incident will come flooding back, uninvited and unwelcome. You have to make the choice not to allow yourself to dwell on it. The more you rehearse the hurtful words and deeds the more indelible they become in your mind.

Choosing not to talk about it. If you talk about it, you think about it. If you think about it, you feel it. If you feel it, it will hurt you.

Choosing not to retaliate. Justice may say, "an eye for an eye", but forgiveness says, "I could, but I won't!"

Choosing to go on choosing. Forgiving is not only a "one-of" act but also an ongoing attitude.

Dwelling together in harmony requires forgiveness to flow freely. No conditions. "If you don't forgive you will not be forgiven. No part of Jesus' teaching is clearer; and there are no exceptions to it. He doesn't say that we are to forgive other people's sins providing they are not too frightful, or providing there are no extenuating circumstances or anything of that sort. We are to forgive them all. However mean, however often they are repeated. If we don't we shall be forgiven none of our own." CS Lewis.

Now is the time. Let the oil of healing forgiveness flow.

A Song to Sing: Psalm 107:1

A Promise to Pursue: John 20:23

A Prayer to Pray: Loving Lord, may forgiveness flow freely all the days of my life, toward me and from me. Help me to live in the joy of Your grace and live by the power of Your grace. To the glory and honor of Your Name, Amen.

Journal jottings:

15

Your Home, a Holy Place?

Exodus 30:25-29

The Tabernacle – an anointed place of meeting and worship. Its utensils and accessories consecrated and set apart as holy. In our place of meeting and worship–our homes–there is much to anoint and consecrate. Consider:

The door posts and lintels. The comings and goings, the busyness of life. We need them to be blessed. That, after all, is the essence of the great promise in Deuteronomy 28:1-14.

The kitchen. So often the heart of the home. Anoint it to be a holy place of godly interaction, amidst the preparing of meals, discussions over scheduling, completing of chores, grabbing of snacks, and cleaning of messes.

Family Room. Pray and anoint it to be a place of fun and laughter, of mutual edification, of vulnerable sharing, and a place to unwind and relax.

Dining room. Fellowship, fun and food with family and friends. Inspiring and educational conversation, healthy humor, hearts and minds open for feeding, as well as stomachs. Anoint it to be so.

Bedroom. A sanctuary. Refreshment, renewal and restoration. Sound sleep - Psalm 127: 2, and intimacy with the Lord and your spouse.

A lofty goal to shoot for? Yes, but that is what the Lord would like our homes to be – set aside, consecrated to Him and for His glory. Anointed to be a sanctuary for us, a place of peace, healing, love and worship.

A Song to Sing: Psalm 48:1

A Promise to Pursue: Joshua 24:15b

A Prayer to Pray: Lord Jesus, may my home be a holy place and place where Your presence if felt by all who enter. May we bring glory and honor to Your Name as we live out our lives within our four walls. In Jesus Name, Amen.

Journal jottings:

16

Anoint Your Sons

Exodus 40:15

Your days are numbered. Sorry to be so blunt, but it is a reality.
The days of our lives are counted, set out; there is a time to be born and
a time to die (Ecclesiastes 3:2). The Psalmist remarks that every day of
our lives was recorded before even the dawn of time (Psalm 139:16).

Living in the truth of these facts can lead to a number of
responses:

Fear- When will my life be over, how will it end?

Panic- There is so much I want to do; how will I ever do it?

Apathy – Well, if all my days are numbered, there is nothing I can do about it. I just do what feels good in the time I've got left.

Of course none of those are sensible or godly.

Our heart should be that in the days we have we'll live them to fulfill God's plan and purpose for our life. To live in such a way that brings great honor and glory to His name.

One vital aspect of a life lived that way is found in our passage – anoint your descendents. We have the responsibility to inspire instruction, encourage and enable the next generation. The mark of success is to raise a successor.

The Psalmist talks of this in Psalm 78:4 "...tell the next generation about the glorious deeds of the LORD....tell of his power and the mighty miracles he did." (NLT). That is precisely what we must do as parents, grandparents, great grandparents, as members of the church. Are we fulfilling this responsibility?

Time passes quickly, days are short. Which members of the next generation can you "anoint" today?

A Song to Sing: Lamentations 5:19

A Promise to Pursue: Daniel 4:3

A Prayer to Pray: My Lord and Savior, please keep my eyes open and my heart ready. Bring to me, members of the next generation, that I might tell them of Your goodness and love. And that the way I live my life will inspire them in their walk with You. I ask this in Your Name, Amen.

Journal jottings:

17

The Great Physician – One

James 5:14

Sickness, there is a lot of it about. Sickness of the body, of the mind, of the heart and of the spirit. From the moment Eve bit into the Apple sickness has been a part of our fallen humanity. It is the reality of life in a sin sick world.

Now of course advances in medicine, including DNA research and technology, have helped tremendously. But everyday illnesses come, lives are changed, suffering increases and death comes knocking. Hospital wards are full, physiatrists' couches are occupied.

That is why we have the marvelous provision of our scripture—the anointing of oil and the prayer of faith. There is nothing special about the oil, no special "magical" ingredient. It is just a symbolic act. However, there is something special, very special about the One in whose Name the prayer is prayed. Jesus, the great physician.

He is the One of whom Isaiah prophesized, "And by His stripes we are healed" (Isaiah 53:5, NKJV). The One who, as He walked the Earth, went around healing all kinds of disease and infirmity. It is He to whom we come.

Oh sure, doctors and hospitals can do marvelous things but ultimately even their ability is from their Creator. Some recognize it, some don't, but it doesn't change the fact.

Over the course of the next few devotions, we'll examine this subject in a little more detail.

But dear one, if you are suffering now, look to the great physician. The One who formed you (Psalm 139:13). He knows every organ, every muscle, every inch of every blood vessel and every inch nerve, every single cell in your body. Consult with Him. No appointment necessary, and He makes House calls.

A Song to Sing: Psalm 59:16

A Promise to Pursue: Isaiah 58:8

A Prayer to Pray: Lord Jesus, You knit me together in my Mother's womb, You saw me while I was yet unseen. Touch my body now, bring Your healing power. For my loved ones to I claim the promise of Your healing power. I pray this in the Name which is above every name of every sickness. In Jesus Name, Amen.

Journal jottings:

18

The Great Physician – Two

James 5:14

Supernatural healing can be a controversial issue. Nothing new of course, it was even for Jesus when He walked the Earth. People questioned (Matthew 12:38), people misunderstood (Matthew 10:12), and people mocked (Matthew 9:34).

The Old Testament prophets had been clear, however. One was coming who would be a healer, the passage in Isaiah perhaps being the most well known. Proclaiming that the healer's blood would be shed by thirty-nine extremely painful lashes (Isaiah 53:5). Provision for healing from each of the thirty-nine categories of disease known to man, at least according to some scholars.

Malachi, too, prophesied, "The Sun of Righteousness shall arise with healing in His wings" (Malachi 4:2). The Hebrew word used here for wings is "kanaph". Meaning an edge or extremity, like the hem of a garment.

An anonymous woman knew this prophecy. Her issue of blood having drained her bank balance and annihilated her friends, she understood it. She understood the Son of Righteousness was now among them, very nearby in fact, in the midst of the thronging crowd. She stood on that promise, pressed through the crowd, reached out, touched the hem of His garment and received her healing. The healer addressed her with these wonderful words, "Be of good cheer, daughter; your faith has made you well" (Matthew 9:22, NKJV). Faith in the Healer through promise of the prophet.

Determined, persistent, faithful; words that very adequately describe this woman. Do they describe us as we reach out through the crowd to the One with "healing in His wings?"

The crowd may try to block us, the crowd may even mock us, but, dear one, stay in faith, press on through to the Great Physician.

A Song to Sing: Psalm 145:11

A Promise to Pursue: Mark 5:34

A Prayer to Pray: Precious Jesus, in faith to You I come, standing on Your word. Heal me, I pray; heal my loved ones, I ask. That all might bring Glory and Honor to Your Name. And I thank You for it. In Jesus Name, Amen.

Journal jottings:

19

The Great Physician - Three

James 5:14

On our television screens, in our magazines, even giant sized on our freeway billboards – are beautiful, perfect, healthy, flawless people. The message – you too can be like them, if only you buy this or do that. Of course, an aspiration out of reach for most of us, and, in fact, for the vast majority of the world's population.

However for followers of Jesus there is a day coming when we will be perfect, complete, 100% fit and healthy, better even than a billboard model. A day when these earth-suits in which we currently reside–with their aches and pains, their cancers and diseases—will be discarded. We'll receive new bodies for our new home, our true home – Heaven (Romans 8:23). How wonderful, how marvelous! Bodies free from sickness, pain, grief, tears and sin. The ultimate healing for us all.

As C. S. Lewis reminds us, "If I find in myself a desire which no experience in this world can satisfy, the most probable explanation is that I was made for another world."

When Jesus healed two thousand years ago, when Jesus heals today, it's like a foretaste of that reality. A little glimpse into a window of a world to come.

As we seek the Great Physician for His healing today, as we act under the provision of James 5:14, we say, Lord Jesus my healer, bring a little heaven to earth today. You are able, I am ready. Let the praying, let the anointing begin…

A Song to Sing: Psalm 147:5

A Promise to Pursue: 1 Corinthians 15:38

A Prayer to Pray: Lord Jesus, as I read the stories of Your healing power being manifest while You walked, as I hear the testimony of healings today, I simply come to You and say strengthen, renew and restore this "earth-suit" I pray. In Jesus Name, Amen.

Journal jottings:

20

Anointed to be King – One

1 Samuel 16

David, so famous, so well known. David the shepherd, the harp player, the giant slayer, the great warrior, the King, the adulterer, the forgiven, the songwriter, the hero. The life and times of David – abundant material for sermons, books, devotions and, yes, even Hollywood.

He captures our attention because he is such an undeniable mixture of the spirituality we aspire to, achievements we aim for, and faults we can identify with. Over the course of the next few devotions, we will again be inspired by him, identify with him and learn from him.

David – the handsome, ruddy, shepherd boy and king man.

It all starts, of course, with an anointing of oil. The word of the Lord comes to the prophet Samuel, "Fill your horn with olive oil and go to Bethlehem"(1 Samuel 16:1 NLT). Samuel's horn, some translations have it as flask, was a piece of equipment a prophet should never be without. It was probably the exact same horn used in the anointing of Saul in 1 Samuel 10. Furthermore, scholars even suggest it would have been the same one used by Zadok the Priest to anoint Solomon in 1 Kings 1:39.

A man of God with a container of anointing oil and obedient to the word of God becomes a tool in the hand of God to launch a ministry that would impact countless generations. Did Samuel have any idea of all that would follow this act of anointing? Probably not, but he started where we all must – obedience to the word of the Lord.

Do you have your "horn" of anointing oil at the ready? Is it in your purse, the glove box of your vehicle, in your desk drawer? Are you prepared for when the word of the Lord comes, the call to pray and anoint someone He directs you to?

I trust so. Who knows what might come forth from that moment.

A Song to Sing: Psalm 105:1

A Promise to Pursue: Psalm 65:4

A Prayer to Pray: Dear Lord, help me to listen for Your command, to be ready for Your word. Is there someone today that will be my divine appointment? Speak, oh Lord, for Your servant is listening. In Jesus Name, Amen.

Journal jottings:

21

Anointed to be King – Two

1 Samuel 16

Samuel and his horn of oil arrive in Bethlehem. A royal city, burial place of Rachael and birthplace of two Kings–David the one he had come to anoint, and also a descendent of David's, Jesus. This little city set among the fertile hills and valleys of Ephrathah. Bethlehem, which means "house of bread", would become birthplace of the One who would call Himself "the Bread of Life."

Jesse a proud father of eight sons and two daughters is asked to assemble his sons for the purification rite. Fine, tall, good looking men, surely great candidates for the office of King. Well, of course, you know the story. The Lord looks at the heart, not the outward appearance. So the call goes out, "Do you have any more sons?"

Jesse's reply is so telling, "There is still the youngest; he is in the fields watching the sheep." Permit me to paraphrase. "Well, there is still the youngest, but he's just a kid. Can't see much potential in him; in fact, we just give him the chores no one else wants to do."

Do you feel that might describe you? Overlooked and underrated. Others around us clamor for positions and honor; we just go about our assignments faithfully, diligently. Yet, somehow, we know there must be more.

Well, there is more. Whether we are nine or ninety, there is a prophet who comes to anoint you—Jesus. He sees our incredible potential, we see our inadequacies. He sees our gifts and talents, we can be oblivious. He sees our heart, we can be too self-critical. As Max Lucado says, "The one who knows you the best, loves you the most." That is very reassuring.

Feel like life might be passing you by? It is not. Your anointer is close by, calling your name, calling you to step up and step forward.

A Song to Sing: Psalm 57:9-11

A Promise to Pursue: Jeremiah 29:11

A Prayer to Pray: Lord Jesus, reveal to me the plans and purposes You have for my life. Show me just a little of my destiny in You. I am Yours. Thank you, that You are mine. In Jesus Name, Amen.

Journal jottings:

22

Anointed to be King – Three

1 Samuel 16

The young shepherd, the kid brother, stuck out in the fields looking after the smelly, stupid sheep. The job nobody wants to do. The short straw David is always stuck with. Yet, what might have appeared as a dead end job was actually a wonderful training ground for the boy born to be king.

A place of preparation for that which was to come, an opportunity for developing gifts and skills so necessary later in life. Consider:

Where did David develop his musical skills as a harpist, as a song writer? Doubtless on a Judean hillside. Idling away the hours with an audience of only sheep, birds and grass. The gifted musician honed his talent.

Sheep have a number of enemies. The most frightening— lions and bears which where a very present threat. A well aimed stone from a sling shot would see them off. Practice makes perfect. A nine foot giant would later prove to be an "unmissable" target.

Long hours, limited company. A recipe for boredom? Not when you have a "heart after God." We can only guess at the sweet precious moments of interaction David must have had with his Lord during those shepherding days. But we do hear the consequence time and time again in the Psalms.

All preparation, indeed, for the greatest King Israel ever knew.

For us, too, God is always at work preparing us for what lies ahead. Perhaps you feel stuck in a dead end job, a loveless marriage, a godless family, a lifeless church right now? Take heart. Unbeknown to you, right now, this just might be a training ground for some glorious dynamic season that is just ahead. To use the modern terminology, "Hang in there."

A Song to Sing: Psalm 23:1-3

A Promise to Pursue: 1 Chronicles 4:10

A Prayer to Pray: Jesus, do Your work in me. Prepare my heart, educate my mind, stir my spirit. I desire to be prepared for all that You have for me. My heart is to serve You and Your Kingdom to the glory and honor of Your Name. Amen.

Journal jottings:

23

Anointed to be King – Four

1 Samuel 16

In addition to being ready to receive the anointing ourselves, we should always be ready to anoint and release others, to be a part of releasing them into their full potential in Jesus. This is one of the greatest joys and privileges of being in the family of God.

Yet, sometimes we can fail to do so, because we are too critical. We fail to see potential in others because we know them too well. Their faults, failings and inadequacies stare us right in the face. We see with human eyes and human understanding rather than with the eyes of a loving graceful, empowering savior. We might say they're too young, too old, too lacking, too fallen.

If we are honest, there may be a little older brother spirit in us. Like David's brothers in 1 Samuel 17:28, "you're not up to this; go home." Or even the prodigal son's elder brother in Luke 15:30, "it's just not fair." Beloved, we must be so guarded against that attitude. Pause for a moment; reflect. Have I ever been that way? If so, seek forgiveness right now.

What we must do is develop a desire to see others fulfill their God given potential. More easily said than done, because, too quickly, we see faults and failings. But we must look for the flowers, not at the weeds. Sometimes we have to discipline ourselves to do so, because it is contrary to our human nature.

So we should be prepared to anoint either by act or prayer:

as parents, for our children to fulfill their potential and know the Lord at a deeper level than even we do;

as husbands and wives, to enable our spouses to walk with the Lord in a deeper richer way;

as church family, to release those around to achieve in God things we've only dreamt about.

Who can you pray for today?

A Song to Sing: Psalm 118:21

A Promise to Pursue: Psalm 33:11

A Prayer to Pray: Lord Jesus, please help me to see others as You see them. Might I look with the eyes of grace to see the potential of all those around me. Then please give me the words to speak to encourage and bless them in Your Name. I pray in Jesus Name, Amen.

Journal jottings:

24

Wars and Battles – One

Isaiah 10:25-27 NKJV

All around us war. Reports and pictures from war zones and battlefields fill our newspapers and television screens. Oppressed peoples and refugees stare out hopelessly while political pundits analyze the latest situation in minutest detail.

Enemies, oppression, battles; all very much part of life in Old Testament times, too. God's people, the nation of Israel, lived in the harsh reality of life under a brutal oppressor. Our scripture shows that help is on the way, the battle will be won, the bondage will be broken, and the war will be over. The anointing of oil will break the yoke (Isaiah 10:27 NKJV).

For us too, wars, battles, oppressions are a part of our daily lives. Some have to do with physical battles of everyday: a belligerent boss, a lying colleague, an untrustworthy employee, a rebellious child, rowdy neighbors, rampant bureaucracy. It's so tiring; we are so exhausted, staggering under the yoke of oppression.

Other battles and oppressions are more obviously spiritual: battling with temptation, fighting an injustice, warring to save a marriage from destruction or a church from a painful split. Behind it all we see Satan's handiwork. Satan, our great enemy, is just that – an enemy. He wars against believers everyday. Jesus said of him in John 10:10, "The thief's purpose is to steal and kill and destroy" (NLT).

Yet, however battle weary and fatigued we are, we must keep this all in perspective. We know the end of the story; we've read the last book of the Bible. We win in the end! Jesus, the Anointed one, the Great Victor will have the final word.

Dear one, feeling a little bruised and beaten, whipped and wounded right now? Do you feel as if the oppressor's yoke has pushed your face into the mud? Take heart; Jesus, the mighty warrior, knows and even now goes to battle for you. And there is ultimately only one outcome: victory, sweet victory.

A Song to Sing: Psalm 98:1

A Promise to Pursue: 1 John 5:4-5

A Prayer to Pray: Lord Jesus, my strong defender, the lifter of my head, into Your victorious hands I place my battles. In my own strength I am weak, but in Yours I am strong and victorious. So be it, Lord, Amen and Amen.

Journal jottings:

25

Wars and Battles – Two

Isaiah 10:25-27 NKJV

The majority of us will not be called to a battlefront in some distant land. Or be recruited to bear arms for some local political cause. However, all of us, every one, engages in a very real war. A spiritual one. Satan, the enemy of our soul, wars against us. He tries to seduce us with temptation, discourage us through circumstances and wear us down with doubts and fears.

As any general will tell you, there is always one strategic place that is the turning point in a war. If that bridge is held or that hill top lost, it can mean the difference between victory and defeat.

Our enemy knows this, too. His biggest battle ground? Our minds. If Satan can influence what happens in our minds that will, in turn, affect our hearts. Proverbs 23:7 puts it like this, "For as a man thinks in his heart, so is he" (NKJV). The Apostle Paul also reminds us of this fact several times in his writings, the most well known being 1 Corinthians 4:4.

There are, however, two very practical things we can do to help protect our minds and guard our thought life:

Examine and evaluate. Experts tell us we have over 10,000 thoughts a day. Some are good, some not. Some are healthy, some are not. What we must do is evaluate them before we act upon them. Quit acting so impulsively. "What Would Jesus Do?" really is a great motto to live by.

Exchange and engage. Trade in the enemy's lies for God's truth. Satan is the "father of lies." We must stay focused on the truth, read our Bibles, pray daily, go to church, be around other believers, and stay close to Jesus.

Take a moment now. What has your mind been dwelling on recently? Are there some pathways your thoughts have led you down that you can see are dangerous roads? Stop. Let the one who "breaks the yolk by the anointing of oil," put you back on track. One more victory chalked up.

A Song to Sing: Psalm 144:1-2

A Promise to Pursue: 2 Corinthians 10:3-4

A Prayer to Pray: Lord Jesus, in the business of the day when a thousand thoughts race through my mind, help me always to stay focused on Your truth and in the flow of Your grace. I place upon my mind the helmet of salvation. In Jesus Name, Amen.

Journal jottings:

26

Our Thorough God – One

Exodus 30:22-25

There are countless adjectives that describe our God. Many are on our lips when we sing our songs of praise and worship on a Sunday morning or as we accompany our radios during our morning commute. We reflect and mediate on these lovely descriptions of our God during our quiet times and devotions.

There is, however, one adjective that less readily springs to mind, but nevertheless is still as true, still as inspiring. That word– thorough. Our God is a thorough God.

Consider our scripture for today: the recipe for anointing oil. Very detailed, very precise, very exact. Nothing left to chance or option. Clear, thorough instructions. That is our God. A "cum-se-cum-sa" attitude He does not have. Consider the very detailed instructions set out in Leviticus, the layout of the Tabernacle, unfolding of the Last Days as given in the Book of Revelation. God is thorough.

Not so the enemy of our souls; he thrives on chaos and confusion, mess and muddle. Oh, how he loves to mess up people's lives, bringing heartbreak, confusion, pain, anguish and rejection! Thankfully our thorough God is always at hand. He who delights in order, restoration and renewal helps us get our lives straightened out, thoroughly, completely.

Feel rather messed up right now? Marriage a mess, family a mess, business a mess, church a mess. Seek the help of the Thorough One. Order, healing, harmony, peace will be the consequence of your seeking.

A Song to Sing: Psalm 135:5-6

A Promise to Pursue: 1 Corinthians 15:58

A Prayer to Pray: Lord Jesus, thank You for loving me thoroughly. Thank You for Your extravagant grace that continues to reach out to me. Holy Spirit, fill me afresh, I pray, wash me, cleanse me, renew me thoroughly. I thank You for it. In Jesus Name, Amen.

Journal jottings:

27

Our Thorough God – Two

Ruth 3:1-7

A young widow, she had suffered much. Arduous journeys, frightening famines, pitiful poverty and to cap it all, the death of her husband. A rather depressing story? Thankfully not.

Of course the story does not end there, not when you love and serve the God of the second chance. A thorough God who leaves nothing to happenstance. A new man, a potential husband comes into the picture. A good catch? Oh yes, doubtless. Upon instructions of her mother-in-law, she does something that appears routine but, in fact, is an insightful act of thorough preparation; she anoints herself.

The anointing speaks of two things.

Firstly, physical. She was a worker, laboring in the field. No walk-in showers for freshening up in those days. You had to make do the best way you could. Anointing yourself with sweet smelling oil was one way. Letting its fragrance mask other less pleasing odors arising from her body. Physical cleansing is still important for all our relationships today—marriages, family, churches. Enough said!

Secondly, this was a spiritual act. Her anointing signified a setting apart. Firstly to the will of God and secondly to her husband to be, preparing to come under his headship and spiritual authority. Seen, too, in the physical act of lifting the corner of Boaz's blanket and covering herself with it.

Thorough preparation by an obliging servant, submitting to the will of a thorough God whose business is restoration.

Are we as well prepared for life's assignments? Are we as obedient? Ask yourself the question; listen for your Lord's reply.

A Song to Sing: Psalm 119:135

A Promise to Pursue: 1 Peter 1:13-16

A Prayer to Pray: Loving Savior, I humbly come to You as a

willing servant. Have Your way in me; have Your way through me. May I always be prepared to answer quickly, "Yes Lord." In the great and mighty Name of Jesus I pray, Amen.

Journal jottings:

28

The Shepherd's Anointing – One
Psalm 23

As we come toward the conclusion of our journey together, we reflect upon one of the most well known references to the anointing of oil found in the Bible, Psalm 23.

This moving song touches our heart and stirs our spirit. Its imagery so insightful, so readily understandable. For centuries it has been read, sung, prayed for many of life's most emotive moments: birth, baptism, marriage and death.

Verse five is, of course, our prime focus, as it relates to our devotions on the subject of anointing with oil. The songwriter, David, speaks of an anointing, a setting apart, a consecration for protection, provision and potential. As a guest being highly honored at a feast.

There are three reminders here for our life as followers of Jesus. We are chosen, we are called, and we are commissioned.

Firstly we are chosen. The apostle Paul reminds us in Ephesians 1:11 that "... because of Christ, we have received an inheritance from God, for he chose us from the beginning..." (NLT).

You were no accident, no evolutionary random event. You were not a product of Mr. & Mrs. Ape. An amoeba is not your distant cousin. You were, in fact, very much chosen; from before the dawn of time God had your birth date circled on His calendar. The Psalmist who reminds us of those facts (Ps. 139:16) goes immediately on in the next two verses to tell us that God is always thinking about us, "How precious are your thoughts about me, O God! They are innumerable!

I can't even count them; they outnumber the grains of sand! "(Ps. 139:17-18, NLT).

Wait; read those words again. Let them really impact you. Yes, the Creator of the Universe thinks about YOU. Precious loving, grace-filled thoughts, too many to count. So, if God had a refrigerator your picture would be on it. If He carried a wallet your picture would be in it.

Jesus put it like this,"You did not choose Me, but I chose you…–" (John 15:16, NKJV).

In the midst of a world of rejection, isolation and abandonment, that's a wonderful message. As David put it, "You anoint my head with oil; My cup runs over" (Ps. 23:5, NKJV).

A Song to Sing: Psalm 23:1

A Promise to Pursue: Ephesians 2:4-7

A Prayer to Pray: Lord Jesus, thank You for choosing me. Help me never to let the wonder of that fact slip from my mind. May my heart daily stir with songs of praise, worship and adoration to You, my Savior, my Redeemer. Amen.

Journal jottings:

29

The Shepherd's Anointing – Two

Psalm 23

Do you remember as a child playing blissfully outside in the yard or on the street, not a care in the world? In fact, you were probably lost in your own little world until you were called. Called, that is, by your mom or dad, "Come inside at once and finish your chores." "Have you really done your homework?" "Time for bed!" When you heard those words reality struck hard. But you had to go; you'd been called.

Sometimes we attribute the same sense of dread when we hear talk of being called by God. "Oh boy, what does He want me to do now?" "I don't really want to be missionary" The old song, "Please don't send me to Africa" rolls around our head. Maybe we feel concern in case we are being called to serve more, give more, witness more.

However, the good news, very good news, is that whenever He calls, He equips. He anoints you for the tasks He has for you. You don't have to do it in your own strength. It doesn't have to be a chore. The Holy Spirit, the power of God living in you, is all you need.

That is why Jesus told a ragtag bunch of very ordinary men and women, "When the Holy Spirit has come upon you, you will receive power" (Acts 1:8, NLT). They certainly did. They changed from a collection of scardy cats into world changers.

Beloved, you are called. I'm not sure to what exactly. You may know, you may not, but whatever it is, you can do it. The anointing is available for you.

There is a voice calling you once again. To borrow a company motto "Just do it."

A Song to Sing: Psalm 23:3

A Promise to Pursue: Ephesians 2:8-10

A Prayer to Pray: Lord Jesus, thank You for calling me. Help me to be ever listening for Your voice and be ready to respond to all that You have planned and purposed for my life. May my ways bring glory and honor to Your Name. May my achievements help extend the Kingdom. May my witness be ever true. May my life song sing to You. In the wonderful Name of the risen Lord Jesus, I pray. Amen and Amen.

Journal jottings:

30

The Shepherd's Anointing – Three

Psalm 23

Assigned a task and equipped for it. Commissioned. Each and every one of us has a God-given commission. Max Lucado puts it like this, "Your life has a plot; your years have a theme. You can do something that no-one else can. Every year is another chapter God fills with plans He has written for you."

Did you catch that? You can do something that no one else can. How amazing, how exciting, how true! You are a unique combination of gifts, talents, anointing, circumstances, situations and spheres of influence. No one on earth has ever or will ever be able to stand in your shoes. There is only one you in all eternity.

Our response to that incredible truth? It should be the same as that of Mary, "I am the Lord's servant, and I am willing to accept whatever he wants" (Luke 1:38, NLT). Are you the Lord's servant? Are you willing?

Thankfully, in addition to being anointed for the task, Jesus promises to be with us. To stay the course along side us. Matthew 28:20, "…be sure of this: I am with you always, even to the end of the age" (NLT). So we don't go it alone. The Anointed One is beside us, even carrying us during the really difficult moments. Just as it says in the old footprints story.

As we finish our devotions, we conclude with this image from verse five very clear before us. A man of God, a man after God's own heart, a man chosen, called and commissioned. His head dripping with the oil of anointing looking toward heaven and saying, "Surely your goodness and unfailing love will pursue me all the days of my life, and I will live in the house of the LORD forever" (NLT).

That, too, needs to be our cry.

A Song to Sing: Psalm 23:4

A Promise to Pursue: James 1: 22-25

A Prayer to Pray: Lord Jesus, thank You for commissioning me. Fill me with Your Holy Spirit that I may complete the task, run the race and finish strong. I seek Your anointing now; place Your oil upon my head. I desire to live for You and fulfill my calling all the days of my life. In Jesus Name, Amen.

Journal jottings:

Pastor C. Neil Sayers

Pastor C. Neil Sayers serves as Associate Pastor of Grace Community Church in Houston, Texas. In addition to traveling internationally with the ministry, he and his wife Joan founded Family Fullness Ministries offering preaching, teaching and counseling on all aspects of family life, parenting and marriage. *www.familyfullness.org*

Neil & Joan reside in The Woodlands, Texas, and are blessed with five grandchildren and two step grandchildren, and have the great privilege of being spiritual parents to many around the world.